WOMEN'S PRO BASKETBALL TODAY

THE HISTORY OF THE CHARLOTTE

STING

JOHN NICHOLS

Published by Creative Education
123 South Broad Street, Mankato, Minnesota 56001
Creative Education is an imprint of The Creative Company

Design by Stephanie Blumenthal
Cover design by Kathy Petelinsek
Production design by Andy Rustad

Photos by: NBA Photos

Library of Congress Cataloging-in-Publication Data

Nichols, John, 1966–
The History of the Charlotte Sting / by John Nichols
p. cm. — (Women's Pro Basketball Today)
Summary: Describes the history of the Charlotte Sting professional women's basketball team
and profiles some of their leading players.
ISBN 1-58341-008-2

1. Charlotte Sting (Basketball team)—Juvenile literature. 2. Basketball for women—United States—
Juvenile literature. [1. Charlotte Sting (Basketball team) 2. Women basketball players.
3. Basketball players.] I. Title. II. Series.

GV885.52.C42N53 1999   99-18894
796.323'64'0975676—dc21   CIP

First Edition

2 4 6 8 9 7 5 3 1

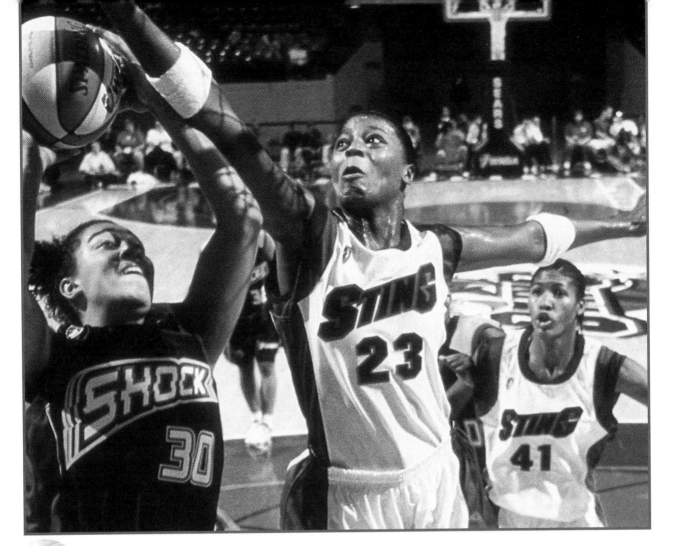

As her 11-foot jump shot arced through the air and swished through the net, Vicky Bullett laid claim to a piece of history. The date: June 22, 1997. The place: America West Arena in Phoenix, Arizona. The opponent: the Phoenix Mercury. Bullett, a 6-foot-3 forward, had just scored the first points in the history of the Charlotte Sting, a charter member of the Women's National Basketball Association. With Bullett's basket, the Sting were off and running as an immediate force in the league. With the stellar play of a platoon of big post players, one of the game's most dynamic guards, and the 1998 Rookie of the Year, the Charlotte Sting have quickly earned a place in the hearts of North Carolina's basketball-crazy fans.

STING PLAYERS SHOW

TEAM SPIRIT (ABOVE);

STING FANS AVERAGED

8,307 IN 1997 (BELOW).

CHARLOTTE—A BASKETBALL HOTBED

The city of Charlotte is situated in the south-central portion of the seaboard state of North Carolina, less than a half-hour drive from the South Carolina border. The city is a perfect example of America's new South; modern big-city skyscrapers share the landscape with lush fields that remind visitors of the area's agricultural past.

One of North Carolina's biggest diversions—some would say obsessions—is basketball. Within the state lines reside some of the best-known college basketball programs in the country. College powers Duke, North Carolina, North Carolina State, and Wake Forest provide the thrills that make basketball the undeclared religion of North Carolina.

In 1987, Charlotte's sports atmosphere graduated to the big time. Local millionaire businessman George Shinn led a campaign that brought a National Basketball Association franchise to Charlotte, and the Hornets have been a success story ever since. In 1995, the National Football League also came to Charlotte when the Carolina Panthers took the field.

In October 1996, Charlotte added to its major-league status when it received one of only eight franchises in the brand-new WNBA, the Women's National Basketball Association. Again, George Shinn was the driving force behind the acquisition. The

VERSATILE GUARD TORA SUBER

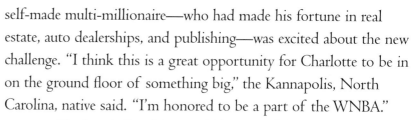

self-made multi-millionaire—who had made his fortune in real estate, auto dealerships, and publishing—was excited about the new challenge. "I think this is a great opportunity for Charlotte to be in on the ground floor of something big," the Kannapolis, North Carolina, native said. "I'm honored to be a part of the WNBA."

Charlotte's franchise would be named the Sting—paralleling its NBA brother, the Hornets—and would play its home games in the Charlotte Coliseum, better known as "The Hive." The first WNBA season would begin in June 1997, shortly after the NBA season ended, and the much-advertised slogan "We got next" let basketball fans know that the women would pick up the action where the men left off.

MEADORS IN CHARGE

With only seven months to build his team before the season tipped off, Shinn knew that picking a top general manager and coach would be crucial. The owner's management team established three criteria for its coach: experience in building a team from scratch, success in coaching Division I college basketball, and the leadership ability to take the team to the WNBA playoffs on a consistent basis.

With these traits in mind, Shinn put Tennessee native Marynell Meadors's name at the top of the list. The 53-year-old had spent 26 years as a head coach in the college ranks and had a sparkling 495–291 record to show for it. She began her career at Tennessee

Tech, where she built the women's basketball program from the ground up. Although her first Tech teams survived on yearly budgets of only $100, Meadors molded the Eaglettes into a fearsome force known as the "Terrors of Tennessee" that stormed through the Ohio Valley Conference on a yearly basis.

Preaching a fast-break offense and aggressive defense, Meadors led Tennessee Tech to a berth in the first-ever Women's NCAA National Tournament. "We had played in the shadows of men's basketball for so long, and we had come so far, it was a great feeling of accomplishment to finally be able to compete in a national tournament," remembered Meadors. "It was a big moment for all of us."

In 1986, Meadors moved on to Florida State University, where she again faced a major building project. FSU was a renowned football school, and other sports—especially women's—received little attention. Undaunted, she quickly transformed the Lady Seminoles from a perennial doormat into an NCAA tournament team in 1990 and 1991.

After leaving Florida State in 1996, Meadors went into broadcasting, but the coaching itch remained. "When I heard there was going to be a women's pro basketball league here in the states, I knew I had to be a part of it somehow," said the hard-driving coach. On March 26, 1997, Meadors was named the Sting's first head coach and general manager. "One of the happiest and

SHARON MANNING (ABOVE);

HEAD COACH MARYNELL

MEADORS (LEFT)

VICKY BULLETT SCORED THE FIRST BASKET IN STING HISTORY.

proudest moments of my life was the day I got this job," said Meadors. "I told Mr. Shinn I wouldn't let him down."

The Sting, under Meadors's leadership, have been far from a letdown. Meadors has taken the franchise to the WNBA playoffs in each of the team's first two seasons. "Coach Meadors demands a lot out of us because she hasn't forgotten where women's basketball came from," explained veteran center Rhonda Mapp. "This is our big chance, and she wants to make sure we take advantage of it."

BULLETT, STINSON HIT THE MARK

When the WNBA plotted out its first season, league commissioner Val Ackerman wanted to make sure that each team would be as competitive as possible. To help create a level field of play, the league decided to assign two top players to each team. "In some cases, we matched players to geographic areas where they had a strong previous history," Ackerman said. "In others, we just wanted to make sure each team had a couple veteran stars to build upon." The Charlotte Sting couldn't have been happier with the two players assigned to them on January 22, 1997: power forward Vicky Bullett and shooting guard Andrea Stinson.

Bullett, who graduated from nearby Maryland University, was an All-American for the Terrapins in 1989 when she averaged

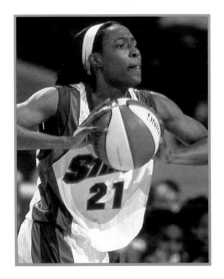

21.4 points and nine rebounds a game. The Martinsburg, West Virginia, native led the school to two straight NCAA tournament

PORTRAIT

NAME: Vicky Bullett

BORN: October 4, 1967 (Martinsburg, W.Va.)

POSITION: Forward

HEIGHT: 6-foot-3

COLLEGE: Maryland '89

Bullett, who scored the first field goal in Sting history, has been a consistent performer in two seasons of play, never missing a start. In 1997 she finished among the WNBA's top 10 in blocks, steals, and rebounds per game, leading her team in each category and finishing behind Stinson in scoring average. The following season, Bullett maintained and even improved her numbers, again leading Charlotte in blocks, steals, and rebounds and finishing third in scoring.

STATISTICS: 758 career points

Year	Average	Total Points	Avg. Rebounds
1997	12.8	359	6.4
1998	13.3	399	6.5

NAME: Andrea Stinson

BORN: November 25, 1967 (Mooresville, N.C.)

POSITION: Guard

HEIGHT: 5-foot-10

COLLEGE: North Carolina State '91

AWARDS AND HONORS: 1997-1998 All-WNBA Second Team, Player of the Week 6-28-98 and 7-14-97, 1997 MVP Runner-Up

Without missing a start in two seasons, Stinson has posted MVP numbers. In 1997, she led the team in points and assists, and scored in double figures in 24 of 28 games. The following season she finished seventh in the league in points, assists, and steals per game.

STATISTICS: 889 career points

Year	Average	Total Points	Avg. Assists
1997	15.7	439	4.4
1998	15	450	4.5

PORTRAIT

appearances. As a member of the U.S. Olympic women's basketball team, Bullett also helped the U.S. bring home gold from Korea in 1988 and bronze from Spain in 1992.

Without a professional league to turn to in the U.S., Bullett played overseas in Italy and Brazil between 1990 and 1996. Deep down, however, she hungered to play in front of friends and family. "It was lucrative and fun to play in other countries, but I wanted to come home and be a part of making women's pro basketball a reality," said the 30-year-old Bullett. "I only wish it could have been sooner in my career."

The 5-foot-10 Stinson came to the Sting after an illustrious college career at North Carolina State University and six seasons of pro ball in Italy and France. Like Bullett, Stinson—who had already been a two-time college All-American and a professional All-Star in Italy—passed up more money overseas to play in the WNBA. "It had gotten to the point where I didn't know if I would play long enough to get a chance here in the states," said the high-scoring guard. "Ending up in Charlotte just made the whole package that much sweeter."

The two veteran stars assumed leadership roles on the team at the Sting's very first practice. "I never worry about Vicky and Andrea," Meadors said. "They give everything they have every practice and every game."

NICOLE LEVESQUE

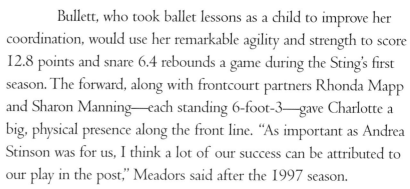

Bullett, who took ballet lessons as a child to improve her coordination, would use her remarkable agility and strength to score 12.8 points and snare 6.4 rebounds a game during the Sting's first season. The forward, along with frontcourt partners Rhonda Mapp and Sharon Manning—each standing 6-foot-3—gave Charlotte a big, physical presence along the front line. "As important as Andrea Stinson was for us, I think a lot of our success can be attributed to our play in the post," Meadors said after the 1997 season.

The explosive Stinson had a monster first season in the WNBA. The North Carolina native finished among the top 10 in the league in scoring (15.7), assists (4.4), and blocked shots (.7), and ranked second in total minutes played (1,011). "Andrea Stinson is relentless," observed New York Liberty head coach Nancy Darsch. "She scores, she rebounds, and she plays defense." The rest of the league would soon take notice of Stinson as well. After leading her team to a 15–13 regular-season record and a playoff berth, Stinson would finish runner-up in League Most Valuable Player voting in 1997.

STING KEEP THE HOME FIRES BURNING

With the outstanding play of Stinson and Bullett paving the way, the Sting proved to be one of the WNBA's brightest lights. After stumbling out of the gate

LOYAL STING

FANS (ABOVE);

FORWARD KATASHA

ARTIS (BELOW)

and losing its first three games on the road, Charlotte returned home to the Hive mad as a hornet. In their first game in front of a home crowd, the Sting pounded the Cleveland Rockers 67–44. Stinson's 19 points and 10 assists, combined with Rhonda Mapp's 11 rebounds, enabled Charlotte to coast to the franchise's first win. "It sure felt good to win one," said a smiling Coach Meadors. "Our fans gave us a lot of energy tonight, and I hope that's something we can look forward to all the time."

Meadors's wish was the Sting fans' command. The basketball-savvy home crowd provided a hostile environment for visiting teams game after game, and Charlotte took full advantage of the support. "Our fans were like having a sixth and maybe a seventh or eighth player on the court," said Meadors. "They were just so good to us, and they did a great job helping to lift us to some victories."

One of the many reasons for the fans' enthusiastic support was the hard-nosed play of such veterans as center Rhonda Mapp. After playing overseas for five years, the North Carolina State alum was elated to join college teammates Stinson and Manning once again and set about earning the respect of the league.

Mapp quickly proved to be a rock-steady presence on the talented Sting roster. Her 1997 season averages of 11.6 points and 5.5 rebounds per game were only the beginning of her

THE STING CELEBRATED A

15-13 1997 SEASON

(ABOVE); ANDREA

STINSON (BELOW)

contributions to the team. "Rhonda does a lot of the dirty work that doesn't show up in the stats," Stinson explained. "Every night, she's in there banging, playing tough "D," and setting screens. It's hard to measure what her attitude means to us."

Following Mapp's hardworking example, other Sting players stepped up their games as well. The guard trio of Penny Moore, Tora Suber, and Nicole Levesque added to Charlotte's offensive attack by combining for nearly 14 points per game while playing heavy minutes.

Energized by Charlotte's tenacious play, the raucous Hive crowd packed the arena on August 16, when the Sting hosted the powerful Houston Comets before a national television audience and a WNBA-record 18,937 fans. The high-profile game featured a showdown between two of the league's biggest stars: Houston's Cynthia Cooper and Charlotte's Andrea Stinson.

Cooper scored the game's first points, but Stinson fired back, canning two quick jumpers to give Charlotte a lead it would not surrender. The Sting received stellar supporting efforts from Rhonda Mapp and forward Andrea Congreaves, who chipped in a combined 31 points, but it was Stinson who stole the show. The sweet-shooting guard tallied 25 points, besting the 17 points of her rival Cooper, as the Sting topped the Comets 80–71. "What a game, what fans, what a day for the league," exclaimed Mapp. "This was what it's all about."

The victory boosted the Sting's record to 13–10 and provided a springboard to the postseason. Charlotte's dominance on its home floor was complete as it finished with a league-best 12–2 home record. On the flip side, however, the Sting's 3–11 road mark was a source of frustration for both the coach and players. "I'm sure some of them were scared to death the first few times [on the road], having never played in front of crowds like that," Meadors pointed out. "When we were in hostile situations, we didn't rise to the occasion."

PLAYOFF FEVER

Despite their fluctuating hot and cold play, the Sting's 15–13 overall record in 1997 was good enough to earn the fourth and final seed in the inaugural WNBA playoffs. For the first season, playoff matchups would be a one-game—winner moves on, loser goes home—affair. "The one-game playoff really boils it down," Bullett said. "Even the best team in the world can have an off-night. If people overlook us, they'll be making a big mistake."

The Sting's first-round playoff opponent would be the mighty Houston Comets. Houston had recovered from the dramatic August 16 defeat suffered in Charlotte and had gone on to post the league's best record at 18–10. League MVP Cooper made it plain that the Comets would not take the Sting lightly. "Charlotte's size gives us real problems, and Andrea (Stinson) is so tough," said the high-scoring Comets guard. "I expect the game to be a real war."

The game was held in Houston at The Summit, and 11,516 screaming fans were on hand to witness a ferocious battle. In the first half, behind the inside power of Bullett and Congreaves, the Sting built a narrow 33–29 lead. The forward tandem hit eight

ANDREA CONGREAVES WAS

THE TEAM'S FOURTH-

LEADING SCORER IN '97.

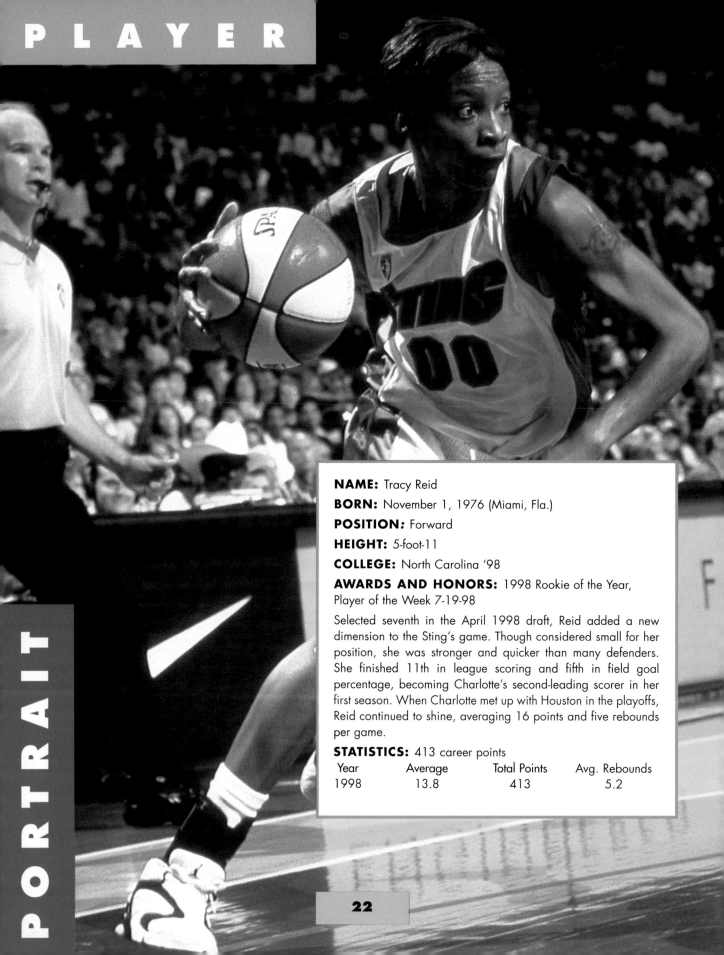

NAME: Tracy Reid

BORN: November 1, 1976 (Miami, Fla.)

POSITION: Forward

HEIGHT: 5-foot-11

COLLEGE: North Carolina '98

AWARDS AND HONORS: 1998 Rookie of the Year, Player of the Week 7-19-98

Selected seventh in the April 1998 draft, Reid added a new dimension to the Sting's game. Though considered small for her position, she was stronger and quicker than many defenders. She finished 11th in league scoring and fifth in field goal percentage, becoming Charlotte's second-leading scorer in her first season. When Charlotte met up with Houston in the playoffs, Reid continued to shine, averaging 16 points and five rebounds per game.

STATISTICS: 413 career points

Year	Average	Total Points	Avg. Rebounds
1998	13.8	413	5.2

NAME: Marynell Meadors

POSITION: Head Coach/General Manager

SEASONS COACHED: 1997-present

RECORD: 33-28

Hired on March 26, 1997, Meadors brought with her 26 years of successful Division I coaching experience. Her coaching career began at Tennessee Tech in 1970, and in her 16 seasons, Tech gained a reputation for running the floor and applying aggressive defense, advancing to postseason play 12 times. Meadors next coached for 10 years at Florida State University, earning Metro Conference Coach of the Year honors in 1990 and '91. In 1992 she was inducted into both the Tennessee Tech and Ohio Valley Conference Hall of Fame. Among all-time coaches, Meadors ranks third in games coached, fifth in total seasons, and seventh in career victories. In Meadors's first season with the WNBA, her Sting went 15-13 before succumbing to Houston in the playoffs. The Sting would requalify for the playoffs in '98, amassing an 18-12 record before once again falling to the eventual champion Houston.

of 11 shots in the first half, including Congreaves's two three-pointers. Cynthia Cooper's 17 points, however, kept the Comets within striking distance.

In the second half, Houston cranked up the defensive pressure on Bullett and Congreaves, limiting the duo to only two points the rest of the game. With the usually high-scoring Stinson contributing only eight points for the game, the Comets went on a 12–0 run to take a 58–48 lead. The Sting battled back, but Houston's dominating 24-11 second-half rebounding advantage was too much to overcome. "It hurt bad because we didn't play our best," said a disappointed Bullett after the 70–54 loss. "We needed to play 40 strong minutes to beat Houston, and we didn't get it done."

The Comets went on to capture the WNBA title, defeating the New York Liberty 65–51, and the Sting headed into the off-season with work to do. "We made a lot of strides in our first year," noted Meadors. "But I think we know now that there's room for improvement."

ROOKIE REID PROVIDES A SPARK

With Vicky Bullett, Rhonda Mapp, Andrea Congreaves, and Sharon Manning, the Sting boasted one of the league's biggest and most physical front lines. But going into the 1998 College Draft, Coach Meadors longed to add some speed to the mix. "When the pace of the game slowed down, we really pounded teams inside with our big people," Meadors observed. "But teams that pushed the ball and ran gave us problems."

With that in mind, Meadors drafted a speedy forward with whom fans from the Charlotte area were already quite familiar. Meadors's choice with the seventh pick in the first round was two-time All-American forward Tracy Reid from the University of North Carolina.

Reid, who averaged 18.8 points and 8.8 rebounds a game during her college career, was a two-time Atlantic Coast Conference Player of the Year. The athletic forward was perhaps best-known

RESERVE DEBRA WILLIAMS (ABOVE); THE STING FAITHFUL (BELOW)

for a pregame ritual in which she would stare into the eyes of her opponents—her way of letting them know that she came to play.

"As a freshman in high school, I didn't want the ball," she recalled. "I was intimidated. My opponents knew it, and after that season, I vowed to change that. The next year . . . I began to make eye contact with my opponent before the game. I'd wish them good luck, but I made sure to check their eyes. That's what gives me an edge."

The 5-foot-11 Reid gave the Sting a definite edge in 1998, hitting for 13.8 points and ripping down 5.2 rebounds per game. "Tracy gives an added dimension in that she can create her own shot when things break down on offense," said Sting point guard Tora Suber. "When all else fails, you can just toss her the ball and get out of the way."

Reid's impact surprised many experts who thought she was too small to compete with the bigger, stronger forwards in the professional ranks. "They said she wasn't tall enough and was too light," remembered Meadors. "Tracy played power forward in college, [but] at 5-foot-11, most people thought she wouldn't be able to get it done. We knew that with Tracy's tenacity, she would be effective no matter where she played."

Allowed to play small forward because of the Sting's abundance of size, Reid overpowered defenders with her strength and

blew by them with her speed. By the end of the 1998 season, Reid had proved all doubters wrong by winning the first WNBA Rookie of the Year award. "It is a great honor to be the first," said an excited Reid. "It's something that will be remembered for years to come."

MAKING STRIDES

The 1998 season would represent another step in the WNBA's progress. With a year under its belt and a solid fan base established, the league expanded from 8 teams to 10 when the Detroit Shock and the Washington Mystics joined the WNBA. The league also lengthened its schedule to 30 games and switched its playoff format to a best-of-three series. "We want our growth to be slow and steady," noted Commissioner Ackerman. "It's very important we make sure every franchise is on solid footing before going forward."

Solid footing would be an apt description of the Charlotte Sting's situation going into the 1998 campaign. The team returned nearly all of its players from a solid 1997 season and added dynamic forward Tracy Reid and slick-passing University of Arkansas point guard Christy Smith from the college draft. "I think we have a better blend of speed and power this year," noted a hopeful Coach Meadors. "I see us as a much more versatile team this year."

TIA PASCHAL (ABOVE);

FREE AGENT CHARMIN

SMITH (BELOW)

Meadors looked like a prophet as Charlotte started out the season red-hot, posting a 7–2 record in the month of June. As a testament to the Sting's balance, five different players led the team in scoring during Charlotte's first nine games. "This year, we don't need Andrea or Vicky to carry us every night," explained Sharon Manning. "We've got a lot of players who can make us go."

With everything seemingly going its way, the Sting squad experienced a tough setback when team leader Rhonda Mapp went down with a foot injury on June 24. With their inspirational center sidelined for three weeks, the team needed a strong effort from backup Andrea Congreaves to stay in the playoff race. The Great Britain native came up big in the clutch, leading the Sting in scoring three times while Mapp was on the mend. Among those performances was a 23-point, 10-rebound showing on July 12 against the New York Liberty and their star Rebecca Lobo. "A.C. has a lot of ability, and it was no surprise when she played as well as she did," said Stinson. "We needed her to keep afloat."

Heading into the late stages of the season, the Sting appeared ready to capture their first Eastern Conference crown.

SHARP SHOOTER ANDREA STINSON

Unfortunately for Charlotte fans, a 1–4 mark down the stretch pushed them into second place in the conference and fourth place in the league at 18–12.

The fourth-seeded Sting would draw the daunting task of trying to take down the defending champion Houston Comets, whose WNBA-record 27–3 regular-season mark earned them the number-one seed. The juggernaut Comets knocked the Sting out of the playoffs for the second year in a row, winning 85–71 in Charlotte and 77–61 in Houston. "That is one great team, and we have to tip our hats to them," Mapp said. "But I'm proud of what we accomplished this year. Don't anybody worry about us. We'll be back, better than ever."

With a talented mix of both youth and experience, the Sting should remain a championship contender for years to come. With such stars as Tracy Reid, Andrea Stinson, and Vicky Bullett leading the way, the Hive may soon be home to the WNBA's queen bees.

ROOKIES SONIA CHASE

(ABOVE) AND POLLYANNA

JOHNS (BELOW)